Roy Rogers
3/11/22

Streams in the Desert

JEFF ROGERS PHOTOGRAPHY, INC.

In honor of those who suffer

This book was created without any commercial endorsements, supplies or support.
Deo est Gloria!

Library of Congress Control Number: 2019936742
ISBN: 978-0-9772400-5-0
Printed in South Korea

Unless otherwise indicated, all Scripture quotations are taken from the Holy Bible, New Living Translation, copyright © 1996, 2004, 2015 by Tyndale House Foundation.
Used by permission of Tyndale House Publishers, Inc., Carol Stream, Illinois 60188. All rights reserved.

Scripture taken from the New King James Version®, copyright © 1982 by Thomas Nelson. Used by permission. All rights reserved.

Scripture quotations taken from the Amplified® Bible (AMP), Copyright © 2015 by The Lockman Foundation. Used by permission. www.Lockman.org

Scripture quotations marked TPT are from The Passion Translation®. Copyright © 2017, 2018 by Passion & Fire Ministries, Inc. Used by permission.
All rights reserved. ThePassionTranslation.com.

Matt and Beth Redman, "Blessed Be Your Name: You Give and Take Away, My Heart Will Choose to Say," (Ventura, CA: Regal Books, 2008), 34.

Jeff Rogers Photography, Inc.
www.JeffRogers.com | jeff@JeffRogers.com
P.O. Box 368 | Lexington, Kentucky 40588-0368

INTRODUCTION

We will all face desert seasons where sadness, grief, isolation and confusion seem to come and overwhelm us. In 2007, I lost my former wife, Sally, to cancer. Although we struggled through surgeries, radiation and chemo, the time came for Sally to get an upgrade. For reasons I will never understand, the Lord chose to give her the ultimate healing. During that time, this Scripture became a life verse for her:

> "When you pass through the waters, I will be with you;
> and when you pass through the rivers,
> they will not sweep over you.
> When you walk through the fire,
> you will not be burned;
> the flames will not set you ablaze.
> For I am the LORD your God..." *Isaiah 43:2,3 NIV*

When I lost Sally, it felt as if my heart was being ripped out. But much to my surprise, something new began to happen. Scripture became more alive to me than ever before. Readings from the Psalms became clearer and more significant; in my grief and suffering the words jumped off the pages. Somehow the unfiltered emotions recorded there touched my heart in a deep and powerful way. They helped me get through my loss and brought healing to my heart.

No matter how deep the winter or how dry the desert may be for you, I trust and pray that the Lord will meet you there while you spend time meditating on this book.

Yet what we suffer now

is nothing compared to THE GLORY
he will reveal to us later.

ROMANS 8:18 NLT

Give all your worries
and cares TO GOD,

for he cares about you.

I PETER 5:7 NLT

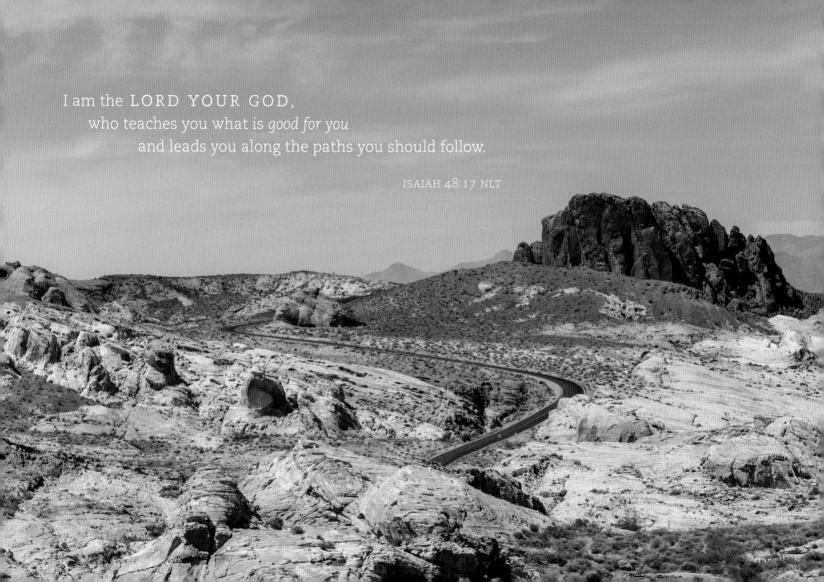

I am the LORD YOUR GOD,
who teaches you what is *good for you*
and leads you along the paths you should follow.

ISAIAH 48:17 NLT

Seek the Lord

while you can find him. Call on him now while he is near.

ISAIAH 55:6 NLT

My fellow believers,

when it seems your are facing nothing but difficulties,

    see it as an invaluable opportunity
    to experience the greatest joy that you can!

    For you know that when your faith is tested
    it stirs up power within you

        to endure all things.

            JAMES 1:2-3 TPT

Who among you fears the Lord
and obeys his servant?

If you are walking in darkness,
without a ray of light,
trust in the Lord and *rely on your God.*

ISAIAH 50:10 NLT

He will not crush the *weakest reed*
or put out a *flickering candle.*

He will bring justice to ALL
who have been wronged.

ISAIAH 42:3 NLT

Worry weighs a person down;
   an encouraging word *cheers a person up.*

PROVERBS 12:25 NLT

Your own ears will hear him.

Right behind you a voice will say,
    "This is the way you should go,"
whether to the right or to the left.

ISAIAH 30:21 NLT

I will answer them before they even call to me.

While they are still talking about their needs,
I will go ahead and answer their prayers!

ISAIAH 65:24 NLT

But he also turns deserts into pools of water,

the dry land into springs of water.   PSALM 107:35 NLT

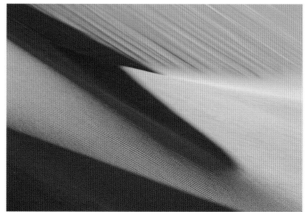

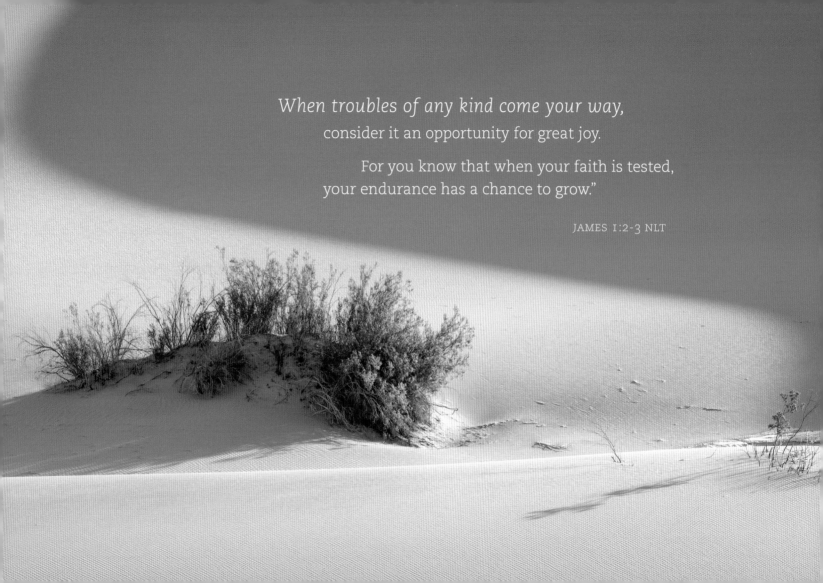

When troubles of any kind come your way,
consider it an opportunity for great joy.

For you know that when your faith is tested,
your endurance has a chance to grow."

JAMES 1:2-3 NLT

Now it will spring forth; Will you not be aware of it?
I will even put a road in the wilderness, *rivers in the desert.*   ISAIAH 43:19 AMP

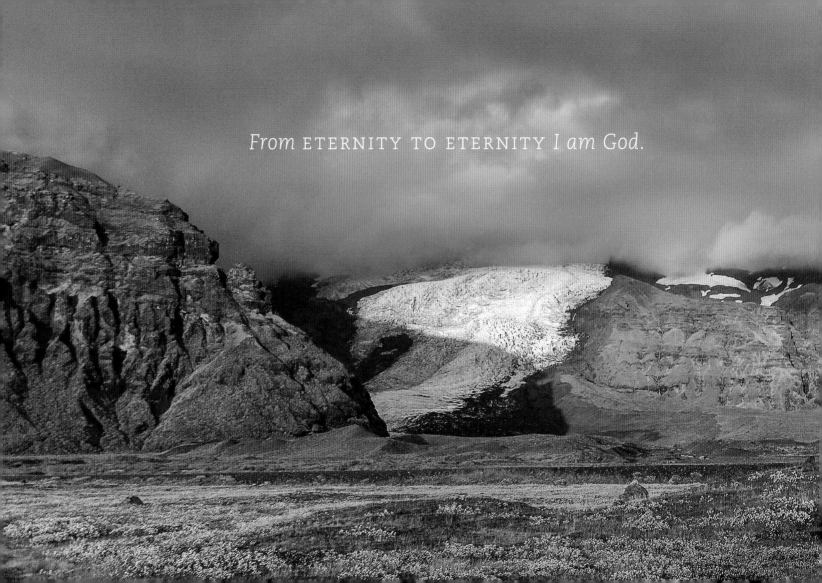

From ETERNITY TO ETERNITY *I am God.*

No one can snatch anyone out of my hand.
No one can undo what I have done.

ISAIAH 43:13 NLT

*For our present troubles are small
and won't last very long.*

Yet they produce for us a glory
that vastly outweighs them
and will last forever!

So we don't look at the troubles we can see now;
rather, we fix our gaze on things that cannot be seen.

For the things we see now
will soon be gone,

but the things we cannot see will last forever.

2 CORINTHIANS 4:17-18 NLT

For since the world began,
  no ear has heard and
  no eye has seen a God like you,
who works for those who wait for him!

ISAIAH 64:4 NLT

Can anything ever SEPARATE US
   from Christ's love?

Does it mean he no longer loves us
if we have trouble
   or calamity,
or are persecuted,
   or hungry,
or destitute,
   or in danger,
or threatened with death?

ROMANS 8:35 NLT

I will *open up rivers* for them
on the high plateaus.

I will give them fountains of water in the valleys.

I will fill the desert with pools of water.

Rivers fed by springs will flow across the parched ground.

ISAIAH 41:18 NLT

He reached down from heaven and RESCUED ME; he drew me out of deep waters.

PSALM 18:16 NLT

He will lead them

to springs of life-giving water.

And God will wipe every tear from their eyes.

REVELATION 7:17 NLT

But blessed are those
who trust in the Lord
and have made the Lord their hope and confidence.

They are like trees planted along a riverbank,
with roots that reach deep into the water.

Such trees are not bothered by the heat
or worried by long months of drought.

Their leaves stay green, and they never stop producing fruit.

JEREMIAH 17:7-8 NLT

Draw near to God,

and he will draw near to you.

JAMES 4:8 NKJV

Don't worry about anything;
    instead, pray about everything.

Tell God what you need,
    and thank him for all he has done.

Then you will experience God's peace,
    which exceeds anything we can understand.

His peace will guard your hearts and minds
    as you live in Christ Jesus.

And now, dear brothers and sisters, one final thing.
Fix your thoughts on what is true, and honorable,
    and right, and pure, and lovely, and admirable.

Think about things that are excellent and worthy of praise.

PHILIPPIANS 4:6-8 NLT

GOD blesses those
who patiently endure testing and temptation.

Afterward they will receive the CROWN OF LIFE
that God has promised to those who love him.

JAMES 1:12 NLT

*The righteous person
faces many troubles,*
but the Lord comes to the rescue each time.

PSALM 34:19 NLT

You can buy two sparrows for only a copper coin,
yet not even one sparrow falls from its nest
without the knowledge of your Father.

Aren't you worth much more
to God than many sparrows?

MATTHEW 10:29 TPT

8

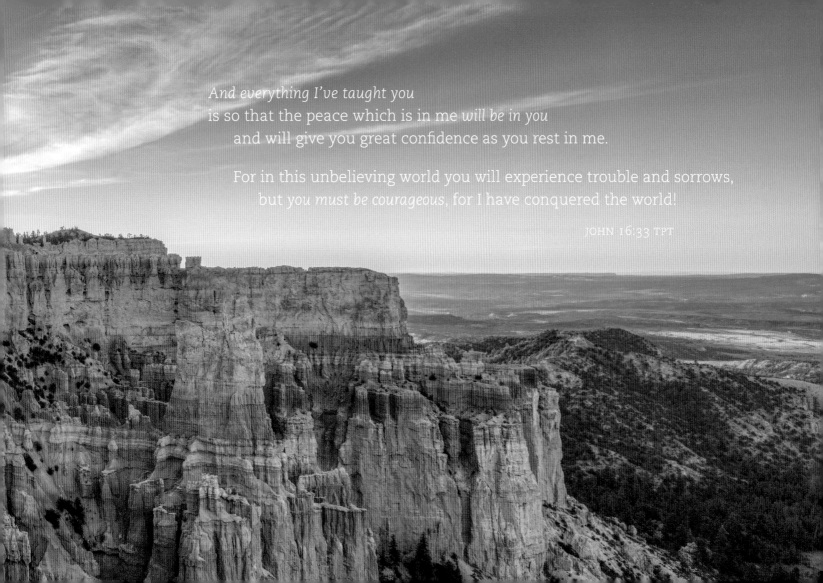

And everything I've taught you
is so that the peace which is in me *will be in you*
    and will give you great confidence as you rest in me.

For in this unbelieving world you will experience trouble and sorrows,
    but *you must be courageous*, for I have conquered the world!

JOHN 16:33 TPT

Darkness as black as night covers
all the nations of the earth,

but the glory of the Lord rises
and appears over you.

PSALM 42:3 TPT

DARKNESS *is my closest friend.* PSALM 88:18 NLT

...wave after wave
You have engulfed me.

PSALM 88:7

Blessed be Your name,
On the road marked with suffering

Though there's pain in the offering
Blessed be Your name.

SONG BY MATT REDMAN

We are pressed on every side by troubles,
but we are not crushed.

We are perplexed, but not driven to despair.
We are hunted down, but never abandoned by God.
We get knocked down, but we are not destroyed.

2 CORINTHIANS 4:8-9 NLT

He will wipe away every tear from their eyes
 and eliminate death entirely.
No one will mourn or weep any longer.

The pain of wounds will no longer exist,
 for the old order has ceased.

REVELATION 21:4 TPT

You will live in joy and peace.
The mountains and hills will burst into song,
and the trees of the field will clap their hands! ISAIAH 55:12 NLT

What happiness comes to you
when you feel your spiritual poverty!

For theirs is the realm
of heaven's kingdom.

MATTHEW 5:3 TPT

But let justice run down like water,
    and righteousness like a mighty stream.

AMOS 5:24 NKJV

Anyone who believes in me may come and drink!
For the Scriptures declare,

'Rivers of living water will flow from his heart.'

JOHN 7:38 NLT

Now, Lord, do it again!
Restore us to our former glory!

May streams of your refreshing flow over us
    until our dry hearts are drenched again.

Those who sow their tears as seeds
    will reap a harvest with joyful shouts of glee.

They may weep as they go out carrying their seed to sow,
    but they will return with joyful laughter and shouting with gladness
as they bring back armloads of blessing and a harvest overflowing!

PSALM 126:4-6 TPT

GOD, THE LORD, created the heavens and stretched them out.
He created the earth and everything in it.

He gives breath to everyone, *life to everyone* who walks the earth.

ISAIAH 42:5 NLT

*I will brighten the darkness before them
and smooth out the road ahead of them.*

Yes, I will indeed do these things; I will not forsake them.

ISAIAH 42:16 NLT

I have swept away your sins like a cloud.

I have scattered your offenses like the morning mist.
Oh, return to me, for I have paid the price to set you free.

ISAIAH 44:22 NLT

For the mountains may move and the hills disappear,
but even then my faithful love for you will remain.

My covenant of blessing will never be broken,
says the Lord, *who has mercy on you.*

ISAIAH 54:10 NLT

He comforts us in all our troubles
so that we can comfort others.

When they are troubled, we will be able
to give them the *same comfort* God has given us.

2 CORINTHIANS 1:4 NLT

DO NOT *be afraid,*
for I am with you. ISAIAH 43:5 NLT

PHOTO LOCATIONS

front cover...Lake Powell, Arizona

5.................................Bryce Canyon National Park, Utah
6, 7................................Winding road through the desert
8, 9.. Zion National Park, Utah
10.. Horseshoe Bend, Arizona
12, 13...................................... Slot canyons, Page, Arizona
14, 15...Rugged terrain in Arizona
16, 17............................... Dry and barren land in Arizona
18.. Phoenix, Arizona
20, 21..Lake Powell, Arizona
22, 23.....................Death Valley National Park, California
24, 25............... Badwater Basin, Death Valley, California
26, 27... Sunset in Iceland
28.......................Death Valley National Park, California
30, 31................Cactus and reflections, Phoenix, Arizona
32...Colors and textures in Arizona
35...Arizona desert
36, 37... Sedona, Arizona
38.. Phoenix, Arizona
40, 41.................................Flowering cactus, Arizona
43.. Phoenix, Arizona

44, 45.................................. Flowering cactus, Arizona
46, 47.................................. Beauty in the desert, Arizona
49.. Phoenix, Arizona
50, 51........ Sunrise at Bryce Canyon National Park, Utah
52........................Sunrise at Acadia National Park, Maine
54, 55.................................. Acadia National Park, Maine
56, 57...Iceland winter drive
59.. Isolation in Iceland
60, 61 ....Isle of Skye, Scotland
62, 63..................Bluegrass and hay in central Kentucky
64, 65..................................Sunflowers, central Kentucky
67.................................. Southern island in New Zealand
68.. Market in Katmandu, Nepal
70, 71.......................... Village in southeastern Nepal
72......................................Barn along coastal Maine
73............ Pemaquid Point Lighthouse, Pemaquid, Maine
75.......................... Sheep lowing in New Zealand
76.............................. Historic church in Iceland
78, 79.....................Portland Head Light, Portland, Maine

back cover .... Phoenix, Arizona